CPS-MORRILL ES

3 24571 0902034 1   516 HEW
Measuring : how big is it?

Note to Parents and Teachers

The SCIENCE STARTERS series introduces key science vocabulary to young children while encouraging them to discover and understand the world around them. The series works as a set of graded readers in three levels.

LEVEL 2: BEGIN TO READ ALONE
These books can be read alone or as part of guided or group reading. Each book has three sections:
• Information pages that introduce key words. These key words appear in bold for easy recognition on pages where the related science concepts are explained.
• A lively story that recalls this vocabulary and encourages children to use these words when they talk and write.
• A quiz and index ask children to look back and recall what they have read.

Questions for Further Investigation

HOW BIG IS IT? explains key concepts about MEASURING. Both imperial and approximate metric equivalents are given. Here are some suggestions for further discussion linked to the questions on the information spreads:

p. 5 *What would you use to measure how much you weigh?* e.g. Bathroom scales.

p. 7 *Can you think of three things you could describe as short, shorter, and shortest?* It might help to explain this using simple objects such as pencils of differing lengths.

p. 11 *In your class, who lives nearest to school?* You could also ask children how they travel to school, i.e. people living farther away may use a car or bus rather than walk.

p. 13 *Which foods make a shopping bag feel heavy?* Vegetables, bags of fruit, cans, and bottles can all be heavy. Encourage children to compare the weight of different objects next time they go shopping, e.g. a big box of cornflakes is surprisingly light.

p. 15 *What other objects would you weigh in tons?* Big machines such as trucks, tanks, and ships, and very large animals such as whales, rhinos, and hippos.

p. 17 *What liquid is put in a car that is measured in gallons or liters?* Gasoline or diesel. Point out the display on a gas/diesel pump that shows how many gallons or liters are pumped into the car and the display inside the car that shows whether it is full or empty.

p. 19 *Which is longer, the length of a football field or the perimeter?* You could ask children to measure a smaller area themselves, e.g. measuring the length and perimeter of a small playground or classroom in paces.

p. 21 *Which do you think is bigger, the area of your hand or foot?* Encourage children to use graph paper to measure this for themselves.

ADVISORY TEAM

Educational Consultant
Andrea Bright—Science Coordinator, Trafalgar Junior School

Literacy Consultant
Jackie Holderness—former Senior Lecturer in Primary Education, Westminster Institute, Oxford Brookes University

Series Consultants
Anne Fussell—Early Years Teacher and University Tutor, Westminster Institute, Oxford Brookes University

David Fussell—C.Chem., FRSC

CONTENTS

4   measure, tall, long

6   compare, size, guess

8   length, inch, foot, centimeter, meter

10   distance, yard, mile, kilometer

12   heavy, light, feel

14   weight, ounce, pound, gram, kilogram, ton

16   liquid, pint, gallon, fluid ounce, liter, milliliter

18   edge, perimeter

20   space, area, square, graph

22   time, speed, heat

24   **Story: The Dress-up Party**
How much chocolate was added?

31   **Quiz**   32 **Index**

© Aladdin Books Ltd 2008
Designed and produced by
Aladdin Books Ltd

First published in
the United States in 2008 by
Stargazer Books
c/o The Creative Company
123 South Broad Street
P.O. Box 227, Mankato,
Minnesota 56002

Printed in the United States
All rights reserved

Editor/Designer: Jim Pipe
Series Design: Flick, Book
Design & Graphics

Thanks to:
The pupils of Trafalgar
Infants School for appearing as
models in this book.

Library of Congress Cataloging-in-Publication Data

Hewitt, Sally, 1949-
  Measuring / by Sally Hewitt.
    p. cm. -- (Science starters)
  Includes index.
    ISBN 978-1-59604-135-6
  (alk. paper)
  1. Mensuration--Juvenile
literature. I. Title.

T50.H388 2007
516'.15--dc22
        2007008636

Photocredits:
*l-left, r-right, b-bottom, t-top,
c-center, m-middle*
Cover tl & tr, 2tl & bl, 3, 6t,
11tr, 13 both, 14 both, 17b, 18bl,
19, 20tr, 21 both, 24-25 all, 26-
27 all, 28 both, 29tr & mr, 30ml,
31br & bl, 32—Marc Arundale /
Select Pictures. Cover tc, 2ml,
6br, 11b, 16b, 31ml—Corbis.
Cover b, 4tl, 5bl, 12t, 15, 16tr,
18tr, 22-23 all, 29bl, 31tr, mr &
bc— istockphoto.com. 44br, 10
both, 12bl—Photodisc. 8—
Corel. 17tr, 18bl—Jim Pipe.
18br—Ingram Publishing. 21
both, 30br—Comstock.

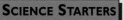

SCIENCE STARTERS

LEVEL

2

MEASURING

How Big Is It?

by Sally Hewitt

Stargazer Books

Heavy weight

Tall skyscraper

How **tall** is that skyscraper?
How heavy is that weight?

Do you sometimes ask
questions like these?

You can find out the
answers by **measuring**.

We **measure** things in different ways.

Tape measure

Tape **measures** and rulers **measure** how **long** or **tall** things are.

Scales **measure** how heavy something is.

• What would you use to measure how much you weigh?

Maya   Jenny   Ben

You and your friends can **compare sizes** when you stand next to each other.

Maya is tall.
Jenny is taller.
Ben is the tallest.

Sometimes you can **guess sizes** just by looking.

Can you guess which of these meerkats is the tallest?

6

You can describe the **size** of something by **comparing** it to something else.

How big is this man?

He's bigger than his dog.
He's smaller than his horse.

• Can you think of three things you could describe as short, shorter, and shortest?

The **length** of something is how long it is. You can use all kinds of objects to measure **length**.

The toy truck is four blocks long. It is also six paper clips long.

How many hands long do you think it is?

It helps if we all use the same measurements.

If we measure a book with different blocks or hands, we get different answers.

So we measure the **length** of a book in **inches** or **centimeters.**

We measure something big like a giraffe in **feet** or **meters.** There are 12 **inches** in a **foot** and 100 **centimeters** in a **meter.**

The height of something is how tall it is.

• Can you measure this book in inches or centimeters, using a ruler?

Distance is how far it is between two places, such as your home and your school.

We measure short **distances** in **yards** or meters. A sprint is a short race that is 100 or 200 **yards** or meters.

A short race

Long **distances** are measured in **miles** or **kilometers**. You can travel long **distances** by car, train, or bus.

Some places are so far away you have to fly there. New York to Rome is 6,800 **miles** (11,000 **kilometers**).

You can use a map to work out the distance between two places.

• In your class, who lives nearest to school?

Big objects are often **heavy**.
A car is made of metal, so it is very **heavy**.
You have to be strong to push it!

These two tubes are big, but they are easy to lift.

They are **light** because they are full of air.

Two objects can look the same size, but they may not weigh the same.

The bag of potatoes **feels heavy**. The bag of popcorn is the same size, but it **feels light**.

A light feather floats down slowly. A heavy marble falls fast.

• Which foods make a shopping bag feel heavy?

There are 16 ounces in 1 pound.

The **weight** of something is how heavy it is.

Kitchen scales measure light objects. They measure **weight** in **ounces** or **grams**.

Bathroom scales measure in **pounds** or **kilograms**. A **kilogram** is a bit more than two **pounds**.

There are 1,000 grams in 1 kilogram.

We use **tons** to measure very heavy objects. This elephant **weighs** 5 **tons**.

There are 2,000 **pounds** (1,000 **kilograms**) in a **ton.** So the elephant **weighs** 10,000 **pounds** (5,000 **kilograms**).
It is too heavy to **weigh** on scales!

• What other objects would you weigh in tons?

We also measure **liquids**. We use a spoon to measure cooking oil or water. To measure larger amounts of **liquids**, we use **pints** and **gallons**, or **liters**.

A sink holds 1 **gallon** (4 **liters**) of water. A pool holds 12,500 **gallons** (50,000 **liters**) of water!

Swimming pool

For small amounts of **liquid** we use **fluid ounces** or **milliliters**. There are 16 **fluid ounces** in a **pint** and 1,000 **milliliters** in a **liter**.

These bottles are different shapes but they all hold the same amount—1 **pint,** or 500 **milliliters,** or ½ **liter**—of liquid.

• What liquid is put in a car that is measured in gallons or liters?

If you run all
the way around
the **edge** of a
tennis court,
you will have
run around the
perimeter.

The **perimeter** is the outside **edge**
of a flat shape such as a table.

**Measuring
the perimeter**

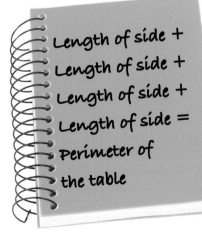

Length of side +
Length of side +
Length of side +
Length of side =
Perimeter of
the table

You can use string to measure the **perimeter** of a shape with curved sides.

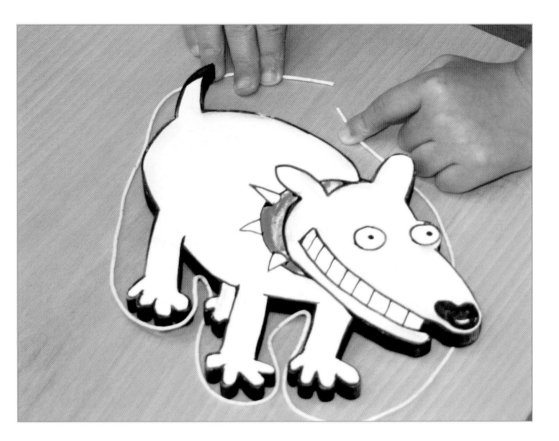

Pull the string around the **edge** of the shape. Cut the string and measure it with a ruler to find out the **perimeter** of the shape.

• Which is longer, the length of a football field or the perimeter?

The **space** inside a flat shape is called the **area**.

We measure **area** in **squares**.

There are lots of little **squares** inside this shape.

Mosaic

Square tiles can help you guess the **area** of a **space** like this kitchen.

Kitchen floor

20

This girl is measuring the **area** of her foot using **squared graph** paper.

Her friend draws around her foot with a pen. She colors in the outlined **area**.

They count the **squares** that are completely or mostly colored in.

The **area** of this girl's foot is about 12 **squares**.

• Which do you think is bigger, the area of your hand or foot?

Clocks and watches measure **time**. School starts at 9 o'clock.

A speedometer measures **speed**. A racing car can **speed** along at 200 miles (320 kilometers) an hour.

Speedometer

A thermometer measures **heat**.
It tells you the temperature.

Water starts to freeze when the
temperature is 32° F (0° C).
You feel very hot when the
temperature is 86° F (30° C).

Thermometer

• Can you remember all the different ways we can
measure objects?

THE DRESS-UP PARTY

Look out for words about **measuring**.

Jeff and Saira were excited.
Aunt Fran was coming to stay.
"Here she is now," said Mom.

"You two have grown!"
said Aunt Fran,
giving them a hug.

"**Guess** how **tall** I am!"
said Jeff. "Um, about
three **feet** (a **meter**),"
guessed Aunt Fran.

"We can show you!"
said the children.

24

They **compared** their **sizes** on their **measuring** chart.

"I'm **taller** than Jeff," said Saira. "And I'm older too!"

They **weighed** themselves on the bathroom scale.

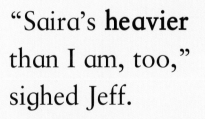

"Saira's **heavier** than I am, too," sighed Jeff.

"It's my birthday on Saturday. I'm having a dress-up party."

"Ooh good!" said Aunt Fran. "May I make the costumes?"

"I'll be a king," said Jeff.
"I'll be a princess," said Saira.

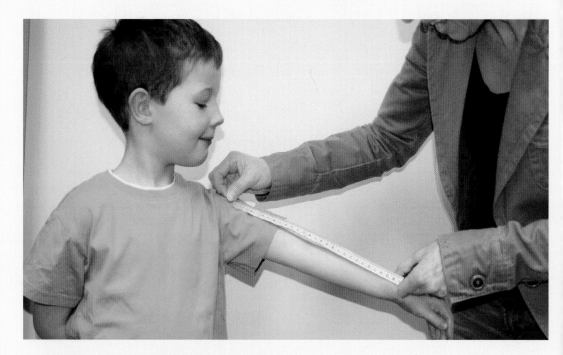

Aunt Fran **measured** the children.
"Now I can make your costumes exactly
the right **size**," she said.

Aunt Fran drew a
pattern using **graph**
paper. "This shows
me the **area**," she said.

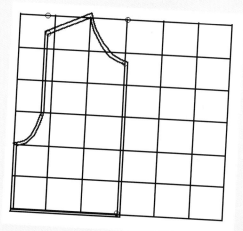

She pinned the pattern to
the material and cut around
the **edges** of the shapes.

Then she sewed the **long**
pieces of material together.

The children
tried on their
costumes.

"Cool!" said Jeff.

"I love my dress!"
said Saira.
"It's just the
right **length**."

27

Some of the guests arrived early. They helped Mom make the birthday cake.

Jeff **weighed** the ingredients on the kitchen scale.

When nobody was looking, Clare put in an extra two **ounces** (50 **grams**) of chocolate chips.

When David helped, he put in an extra two **ounces** (50 **grams**) of chocolate chips too!

Mom turned on the **heat** and put the cake in the oven. Aunt Fran filled a pitcher with juice.

"This **feels heavy**," said Jeff.

"Two **pints** (one **liter**) of juice is about enough for 8 cups," said Aunt Fran.

When all the party guests had arrived, everyone played games in the yard.

There was plenty of **space** to run around fast.

29

"**Time** for cake!" called Aunt Fran. They all sat at the table. Mom brought in the cake.

"This cake **feels** like it **weighs** a **ton!**" she said. "What did you children put in it?" David and Clare giggled.

Everyone agreed it was the best chocolate cake they had ever tasted.

Cut out and color 5 outlines of your foot. Stick them on a long strip of paper.

Now use this to **measure** things around your house, such as a dog or teddy bear.

This dog is 3 "feet" tall

QUIZ

What do we use to **measure** how **heavy** something is?

Answer on page 5

What do we **measure** **long distances** in?

Answer on page 11

What does a thermometer **measure**?

Answer on page 23

Which of these things would you measure in tons, which in pints or liters, and which in pounds or kilograms?

Have you read this book? Well done! Do you remember these words? Look back and find out.

INDEX

A
area 20

C
centimeter 8
compare 6

D
distance 10

E
edge 18

F
feel 12
fluid ounce 16
foot 8

G
gallon 16
gram 14
graph 20
guess 6

H
heat 22

heavy 12

I
inch 8

K
kilogram 14
kilometer 10

L
length 8
light 12
liquid 16
liter 16
long 4

M
measure 4
meter 8
mile 10
milliliter 16

O
ounce 14

P
perimeter 18

pint 16
pound 14

S
size 6
space 20
speed 22
square 20

T
tall 4
time 22
ton 14

W
weight 14

Y
yard 10